Making Ends Meet at the Margins?:
Grappling with Economic Crisis and Belonging

in Beitbridge Town, Zimbabwe

Author

Rekopantswe Mate is a lecturer at the University of Zimbabwe, Department of Sociology. Her research interests hover around issues of identities in societies going through a lot of socio-economic change such as present-day Zimbabwe. She is currently doing research on youth sexuality in the face of HIV and AIDS looking at how youths perceive and respond to this scourge in the face of socio-economic crises.

Making Ends Meet at the Margins?: Grappling with Economic Crisis and Belonging in Beitbridge Town, Zimbabwe

Rekopantswe Mate

Monograph Series

The CODESRIA Monograph Series is published to stimulate debate, comments, and further research on the subjects covered. The Series will serve as a forum for works based on the findings of original research, which however are too long for academic journals but not long enough to be published as books, and which deserve to be accessible to the research community in Africa and elsewhere. Such works may be case studies, theoretical debates or both, but they incorporate significant findings, analyses, and critical evaluations of the current literature on the subjects in question.

This work is a product of CODESRIA's Comparative Research Network on Globalisation, Citizenship, and Xenophobia in Botswana, South Africa and Zimbabwe.

Layout by Hadijatou Sy Sané

Cover designed by Ibrahima Fofana

CODESRIA Monograph Series
ISBN 978-2-86978-152-8

CODESRIA would like to express its gratitude to African Governments, the Swedish Development Co-operation Agency (SIDA/SAREC), the International Development Research Centre (IDRC), OXFAM GB/I, the Mac Arthur Foundation, the Carnegie Corporation, the Norwegian Ministry of Foreign Affairs, the Danish Agency for International Development (DANIDA), the French Ministry of Cooperation, the Ford Foundation, the United Nations Development Programme (UNDP), the Rockefeller Foundation, the Prince Claus Fund and the Government of Senegal for support of its research, publication and training activities.

Contents

Introduction

Debates about entitlement to national resources in Zimbabwe have been framed in two different ways. On the one hand the language of 'national unity' implies that all nationals benefit from national resources equally. This became particularly important after the 1987 Unity Accord born out of violent post-independence ethnic conflict also referred to as the Fifth Brigade atrocities in Matabeleland region, home to most of Zimbabwe's ethnic minorities (see Catholic Commission for Justice and Peace in Zimbabwe [CCJP] 1997). However in the 1990s the austerity of economic reform saw the term Zimbabwean being qualified in calls for 'indigenisation' in which black Zimbabweans or 'indigenes'' (see Harnishfeger 2004) got preferential treatment in economic development. Through numerous black empowerment bodies, discourses of indigenisation seemed to portray blacks as united, homogenous and similarly marginalised in the economy. In reality only a small clique of the well to do seemed to amass wealth while the rest of blacks remained 'marginalised'.

These national perspectives ran concurrently with the policy of decentralisation implemented few years after independence in 1980 in order to make the state more accessible to black people in rural areas especially. However with neoliberalism in the 1990s decentralisation also meant that districts as local authorities responsible for local development would raise their own revenue from locally available resources in order to develop their own regions to augment dwindling allocations from central government. Although it had been envisaged that local authorities would be able to attract donor funding, local and foreign investors, this did not happen due to changes in Zimbabwe's relations with the donor nations. Most local authorities have had to make do with limited government support and equally limited local revenue bases at a time when expectations from local authorities mounted in the face of depeening poverty, increased urbanisation, unemployment among others. It is also during the 1990s, a time of deepening resource austerity that notions of 'outsiders' and 'locals' became prevalent in regions, which because of sought after resources saw an influx of immigrants. 'Locals' are seen as entitled to real and imagined local resources pitted against 'outsiders', immigrants from other regions/districts who invariably are seen as 'poachers, 'squatters', 'deviants' who illicitly or illegitimately access local resources at the expense of indigenes. Tension and conflict over access to land in resettlement areas such as Gokwe now reputed as a cotton farming area have seen intense competition over arable land (Nyambara 2001) or over the establishment of safari areas for purposes of raising income from local wildlife, meaning some people must be moved from their homes (see Hammar 2001; Dzingirai 1995). The local-outsider divide also coincides with ethnic differences (see also Worby 1994; Dzingirai 1995; Hammar 2001; Madzudzo and Dzingirai 1995).

Officially, reference to regions of origin and ethnicity as criteria for accessing resources is seen as divisive and a threat to the social entity called Zimbabwe. It is a reminder of the violence of the post independence era which some would rather forget and others wish to remember as a moral debt which is paid only through revisiting history, apologies to wronged parties and other means of redress (see Werbner 1995). Within this context this paper looks at the emergence of notions of locals and outsiders; deserving and undeserving, entitled and non entitled people in the impoverished town of Beitbridge whose most salient resource is the border with South Africa which is perceived to be a harbinger of wealth through work, theft or the use of zombies and goblins believed to increase one's wealth.

Why Beitbridge?

I first visited Beitbridge in February 1990 to fill 'resumption of duty forms' after being recruited as a temporary teacher in a poor rural primary school in the district. With its untarred roads, unpaved bus terminus, dustiness, ubiquitous litter, pole-dagga-and-thatch huts near the bus stop, animal drawn carts, few shops and numerable taxis the word 'town' seemed anomalous in describing Beitbridge. It was different from Zimbabwean towns I knew.

I returned to the town in the last quarter of 2002 whereupon I was warned not to attempt to walk to any place on my own if I arrived after dark but to get a taxi.[2]

Muggings and violent crime including murder had become common especially at night. Routinely people were picked up dead in the morning with deep cuts.

Upon arrival I was shocked at the sense of crowdedness that I got. Despite my night arrival, the town bustled with human activity with the bus terminus as its epicenter. The dirt, dust and litter were still there but this time mounds of uncollected rubbish could be seen at people's gates. In the ubiquitous litter, used and unused condoms were quite prominent too including right at the gate of the hospital (fieldnotes October 2002). There were more taxis, homemade pushcarts pushed by young men to ferry luggage for those people who could not afford taxis. There were touts to assist people to illegally cross the border into South Africa. These touts mob buses to interest travelers in their services thereby increasing one's sense of vulnerability and confusion in the clamour, shoving and pushing for potential business.

During the day I noticed unkempt young men (some with torn clothes) sleeping on the grass at major service stations while others milled around at the customs and immigration complex looking busy, running this way and that way. I was told that these are hustlers and self-styled travel consultants (magumaguma) who make a living from border activities. There were also young women hanging around truck stops and the border complex. I was told that most such women were likely to be commercial sex workers waiting for potential clients such as travelers and commercial truck drivers. At night the major service stations became a large open space bedroom for men and women alike. Some of these people are 'homeless' others are travelers in transit. When I asked a taxi driver I befriended about what looked like a drastic change from what had looked like a sleepy little town in 1990 to one whose size had not changed but looked abuzz with human activity around the clock and overflowing with people in 2002, he explained that the people who milled around were 'people from the east' whom he claimed had come to the town to 'grab' opportunities from locals in Beitbridge. Throughout a two-week long stay in 2002, casual conversations yielded this explanation of 'outsiders' coming to degrade Beitbridge and its residents by increasing crime, insecurity, prostitution, HIV and AIDS and accommodation shortages. Memories of my 2002 stay in Beitbridge prompted this study, in 2003. Its objectives are to ethnographically show popular constructions of 'outsiders' as non-belonging and not entitled to local resources/opportunities versus 'locals' who belong and are entitled to local resources in a context in which nationally, resources and opportunities have shrunk and regional governments are supposed to concentrate on local development using locally available resources.

A detailed description of Beitbridge town

Beitbridge town is situated in a district of the same name. Historically the district and town were predominantly Venda and Shangani speaking although the latter was (and still is) generally considered a subordinate language/culture due to colonial perceptions and their imprint on current ethnic relations (see Worby 1994). The district is part of Matabeleland South and lies south of Zimbabwe alongside the border with South Africa. Beitbridge district lies in a large swathe of a low lying, hot, low rainfall, chronically food deficit agro-ecological region. Beitbridge district is one of Zimbabwe's poorest. Crop production is impossible without irrigation. The town's hinterland has numerable fruit, game and cattle farms run by companies and individuals. Cattle ranching and game production do better albeit supplementary feeding is necessary if the former is to be viable. Thus the agriculture sector has been one of the largest employers but it is also associated with very low wages and some of the poorest employees. It employs the most desperate individuals in Zimbabwe and even then these people can hardly reproduce themselves from their earnings (see Rutherford 2001). Most local residents, especially males, migrate to South Africa as a result. According to informants common languages and cultures render Zimbabweans from this district easily assimilated into Limpopo province, the South African province adjacent to Beitbridge. Women are left to take care of houses in town or rural homesteads, cattle and children. FHI (2003) observes that 60 percent of the population is female as a result. Depending on the availability of and nature of work, migrant men send remittances in South African currency. Migrants visit during public holidays especially Christmas at the end of the year. Their male children are also likely to migrate to South Africa as soon as they finish primary school. Lately, though, females are also becoming migrants.

The town has an official area of 50 square kilometers. In 1992, its population was estimated at 31 500 people housed in 3 500 housing units. This means on average almost 10 people per house. In other words the town was already overcrowded as far back as the 1990s. Currently, town officials estimate the population to be around 200 000 still housed in the same housing units since there has been insignificant housing development since 1990. The houses are small (three or four roomed) units and cater largely for people employed in the formal sector working for private and public sector organizations.

The bulk of Beitbridge residents live in what FHI (2003) describes as 'the worst houses'[3] in Zimbabwe, the ones which in 1990, my inexperienced mind labeled as incongruous with a town. The pole-dagga-and-thatch settlements

4

emerged as a result of delays in servicing residential plots sold to residents by the town council. These huts are referred to as 'baghdads'[4] or Tangwenas. The huts were meant to be temporary structures pending the construction of approved houses. These huts have become a source of income for the owners of the residential plots as they are leased out to people with no accommodation but live in Beitbridge. They also cater for the growing population of people in transit. The huts do not have water borne sanitation. Residents buy water from people with access to tap water. For toilets some use the bush (there is a nearby forested area which also serves as a source of wood fuel for the residents) while others use public toilets at the bus station or toilets at business outlets such as bars and nightclubs. This explains the pungent stench of 'sewerage' which hangs over the town depending on wind direction. (Some of the smell is a result of a challenged sewerage system susceptible to bursts). Because most people who live in baghdads/Tangwenas make a living from legal (albeit considered as morally suspect and illegal) income generating activities, this settlement is stigmatised for its low housing standards and the deviant livelihoods of its residents. An employee of the town council described the baghdads as 'an eyesore'. Whatever the nature of livelihoods, they orbit around the border post which is seen as a source of opportunities from which livelihoods are drawn.

Beitbridge under SAPs

FHI (2003) describes Beitbridge as the 'barometer' of socio-economic crisis in Zimbabwe. Since the South African economy is considered to be ten times stronger than that of Zimbabwe, fluctuations traffic at the border post speak volumes about pressures in Zimbabwe's economy and the tone of relations between Zimbabwe and South Africa.

South Africa's transition to democracy in 1994 saw an increase in trade with its northern neighbours. 1994 also marked the fourth year of neoliberal economic reform in Zimbabwe where increasing poverty rendered both internal and international migration an emerging livelihood strategy (see Gaidzanwa 1999; Potts 1999). Beitbridge border post reportedly became Africa's busiest, in terms of volume and value of goods; and human and vehicular traffic passing through it. An estimated 7 000 truckers pass through this border post per month most of them spending several days to more than a week waiting to clear goods (FHI 2003). On average 250+/- commercial trucks pass through the border daily with peaks at the end and beginning of the month, while hundreds more are held up on either side of the border pending paper work to clear goods. The border operates 24 hours round the clock every day of the year.

Increased migration from Zimbabwe saw unprecedented demand for passports. The passport office network nationwide could not cope leading to a lengthy time lag (six months to a year) between application submission and issuance of passports. With passport application fees increasing, long waiting periods for passports and the general bureaucratic harassment encountered when applying for a passport, insurmountable and frequently changing conditions for visas[5], a growing number of Zimbabweans became adept at border jumping or passport scams all in a bid to get to a country of choice.

According to informants since the 1990s, there has been an influx of internal migrants wishing to cross the border illegally into South Africa. Some people succeed while others are unable to get the necessary money to pay self styled 'travel consultants' (locally called magumaguma) who assist the desperate with information on how to cross the border illegally or personally guide them through bush tracks in the night. Those who succeed to cross the border illegally risk deportation by South African officials who hand over deportees to Zimbabwean police in Beitbridge. Deportations have increased since 1994. In 2003 the build up to 2004 elections in South Africa was also attributed to increased deportations. The deportees are usually without means to return to their homes in interior Zimbabwe after a hasty departure in South Africa or because they are deported conveniently before their wages are paid. The Government of Zimbabwe is unable to provide assistance through its Social Welfare department which runs its social protection program. Over the years its budget has been rendered too small in the wake of deepening poverty, the AIDS scourge and cyclical droughts. Thus ex-deportees are stuck in small, under resourced and impoverished Beitbridge. Those intending to cross the border illegally are also similarly stuck as they wait for an opportune time to raise the money to bribe their way into South Africa. These people are themselves dispossessed, unskilled and in competition with one another in whatever marginal forms of employment and misemployment (theft, informal trade of different forms and prostitution) to raise money to go/return to South Africa; for one's upkeep in the interim or to remit to expectant families back home.

Research methods and the field situation

Because this study sought a contextual understanding of the construction of outsiderness-localness in Beitbridge, qualitative methods were preferred (Strauss 1987). This meant using semi-structured interviews in the form of conversations about how they identify themselves, the work the respondents did; their experiences living in Beitbridge, how they came to live there, where they lived prior to Beitbridge and how they view inter-group relations in the town and so on. Respondents were identified through snowballing. At first we identified 'a guide', someone who knew Beitbridge well having lived there all her life. Our guide was a woman in her 40s who is quite prominent in the town. She was the first respondent and through her we identified people she described as locals and outsiders. Through them more people were identified. At all times we asked respondents to describe how they could tell outsiders and locals apart.

Security clearance for the study was sought (from several security branches) with an explanation that the study sought an understanding of the effects of migration[6]. We felt that a more detailed explanation that the study sought an understanding of issues of belonging and/or xenophobia might have been considered very sensitive. Worby (1994: 391) explains this jitteriness well when he says: '...[In Zimbabwe] ....tension persists over what may or may not be said with regard to ethnic differences-particularly across the Shona-Ndebele divide'.

Officially, discrimination, particularly on the bases of ethnicity is non-existent and is not condoned yet it persists. People do not talk openly about it either for fear of being accused of fanning ethnic divisions although they do so amongst themselves. Fear of being accused of being a rubble rouser seems very widespread. For instance, it was difficult to identify a willing research assistant as most postgraduate students who can speak languages spoken in the region felt uneasy and feared that they could be seen as rubble rousers by the political establishment.

In the field, my ability to speak languages spoken in the region, (Shona, Ndebele, Sotho and halting Venda) was an advantage which, I think made respondents feel at ease. Some asked questions about where 'I come from' which was quite ambivalent implying either my patrilineal origins and/or where I came from while doing research. I answered it either way without following any set criteria. Given my being multilingual, I sensed that people perceived me to be whomever they wanted/imagined me to be, depending on where I said I came from and the language used in the interview. Often they proceeded to speak as if I understood or was expected to understand their points of view. It was as if I 'belonged with them'. As noted by Kellner (1992:143-154) identity is about perception, construction, presentation and is created from available roles and materials which makes it fragile. My identity in the field cut across the divides I describe below. Because of the fluidity of my identity I think this gave respondents assurances to open up. In this sense, then, there could be biases emanating from our (my research assistant and me) interactions with the respondents. However the issues raised are also debated in private by a lot of people of the many different combinations of identities raised here.

Differentiating Between 'Locals' and 'Outsiders'

Language, mannerisms, accents and family names

Informants consider Venda, Shangani, Sotho and Ndebele as 'local' languages. Unlike the first two which are indigenous to the district (see Worby 1994), Ndebele is learnt at all levels of the school system in the Matabeleland region where the district is found. Sotho is spoken in a neighbouring district and phonetically close to Venda. 'Locals' claimed therefore that they are multilingual which makes them more hospitable. They speak or comprehend at least one 'local' language, in addition to a mother language as well as Shona which is increasingly the language one hears on the streets of Beitbridge although still considered a 'non-local' language. However, it was noted that some people from rural areas might speak only one language Venda or Shangani because of limited exposure to other languages. Such people's localness is defined by being indigenes of the district unlike outsiders who came from elsewhere, or mavhakule which is Venda for 'those who came from far'. Respondents also indicated that locals' names, workplaces, occupations and character are known to their neighbours.

By contrast 'outsiders' are referred to as 'people from the east', or 'these people' and known for their inability or arrogance when it comes to speaking 'local' languages. Reference to the east is an oblique way of saying Shona speaking people or people from Mashonaland. Apparently when spoken to in Venda or Ndebele they respond by saying 'Handinzwi' which is Shona for 'I do not understand'. 'Locals' expressed frustration at outsiders whose attitude was apparently forcing 'local' languages underground since Shona is spoken everywhere in the streets and in informal sector transactions in Beitbridge. One 60-year-old man who says he is 'a local' asked rhetorically that 'are we stupid to learn their language?' Some respondents also pointed out that one can tell locals from outsiders through accents. Although locals can speak Shona and/or Ndebele they often do so with a distinct accent when pronouncing some words which tells them apart as non native speakers. Venda and Shangani are learnt in primary school but in secondary school pupils switch to Ndebele. Some do not learn it well. Shona by contrast is generally learnt on the street and from neighbours. Respondents who claimed to be 'locals' said that outsiders can also become locals after staying in Beitbridge for a long time when they become bilingual and might have a known address and be 'known' to neighbours.

Failure of outsiders to learn local languages is perceived as a death knell for local culture. 'Local' informants noted that in spite of patrilineal norms in which men confer identities such as language and family names to their children, when 'local' men marry 'outsider' women children end up learning their mother's language (Shona) as opposed to their father's. It was noted that because locals can speak other languages, they speak with their in-laws in Shona as a sign of respect and accommodation. This makes it difficult for the women to learn local languages. In the long term, this neutralises patrilineal ideals making Venda men less able to determine their children's cultural identities according to informants. 'Locals' said this is unfair as it denigrates their languages and culture. They felt that their language was shunned by younger generations as a result. They asked rhetorically why they have to learn other people's languages when they go to major towns like Bulawayo (Ndebele) or to Harare (Shona) while people from these places do not learn Venda when in Beitbridge?

Connected to language are mannerisms and symbols of respect, deference and so on. Because Beitbridge is a small town with a large rural hinterland, it is common for rural people to get into town and still continue with rural mannerisms. For instance, when a woman addresses elders of the opposite sex or in-laws, she is not expected to do so while standing. She should crouch or bend her knees deeply and should not look the person in the eye. Women have to put their hands together as if in a Christian prayer and maintain this composed position until the greetings are finished. In-laws are expected to maintain social distance between each other and, depending on the relationship, should not sit in the same room and certainly not on stools or chairs while in each other's presence. Older women who have sons-in-law should always wear something over their shoulders (like a jacket or jersey) or a belt/sash across their shoulders going to the waist when in public in case they come across the son-in-law, his brothers/cousins or his friends who are all classificatory sons-in-law. However, 'outsiders' are said not to be sensitive to these rules of distance, avoidance and symbols of respect. Knowledge of these cultural rituals also differentiates 'locals' from 'outsiders'. In this sense 'outsiders' were alleged to be impolite, brash and discourteous. Of course, outsiders also have their own ways of showing respect. However because most of them are away from home and from relatives, they are under no pressure to show respect even in their own ways. Thus, there is no forum to display their forms of respect.

In addition respondents said that they knew locals by markings on the face common among older people. In the past Venda speaking people and their Sotho neighbours made markings on the face for aesthetics. In some cases they were made for the traditional treatment of eye infections. These markings were made by using a razor blade or some sharp instrument making two or three parallel vertical lines on the cheeks, about two centimeters below the eyes. The lines are not longer than one centimetre. This practice is not common now so that among those below 40 years one rarely sees these markings.

Locals are also likely to have local family/clan names like Muleya (or Mleya), Ndou, Mbedzi or other Venda clan names while Chauke and Mlilo are common Shangani clan names. Within this context many locals also share similar rural backgrounds, chieftaincies and villages. Because Beitbridge has few schools most professionals who originate within the district would have been educated in same schools within the district (namely Tongwe, Vembe or Zezani) or in neighbouring districts. Where the individuals are educated elsewhere people still fall back on rural background, genealogy and chieftaincies to differentiate between locals and outsiders.

We asked government officials (officials of a government line ministry which is mandated to 'create employment' by giving funds to individuals with potentially viable income generating projects) how they deal with the 'local'-'outsider' differences in their work. Funds for income generating projects are given by central government and are distributed at district level where citizens of the district should benefit in keeping with the policy of decentralisation. Officials said they use the criterion of addresses and if in doubt applicants must be 'known' or prove to have lived in Beitbridge for a long time. Usually because loans require witnesses, there must be someone to vouch that the information given in the application form is true. Officials conceded that it is a lot easier to discern 'localness' in rural areas than in town. In the latter, people can connive with witnesses to present false information. Officials said from a government department point of view, they could not deny loans to people whose claims are tight even when they know that the person comes from elsewhere without risking accusations of discrimination. What matters is the applicant's ability to pay back the loan. It is assumed that a fixed address in the town or within the district means that the applicant is less likely to run away with the loan.

Although 'locals' defined Shona speakers as 'outsiders', some of the latter defined themselves as locals arguing that they have lived in Beitbridge for a long time, have friends from all walks of life and ethnic groups in the town. They emphasised having a residential address in the town as a definer of localness. One young man originally from Masvingo said:

> ...If you are not of fixed abode ('somewhere to live') within the district how can you be local? It is important to have an address'. In Shona he said

'....kana usina pekugara muno ungagoti uri mugari wepano sei? Adresi inodiwa'.

He calls himself a 'local' because his father worked for the railways and was stationed in Beitbridge and has a house in the town in which he lives. He went to school in the town.

Outsiders who could not speak local languages attributed this to time constraints, because of spending more time 'working hard' and that they were in Beitbridge '...to make money and not to make friends'. Some said they were only in transit so there was no need to learn local languages. Others wanted to separate themselves from locals accusing them of being 'lazy' and 'envious' and wont to inform the police of their business activities in order to get them arrested. One foreign currency changer said learning the local language depends on length of stay and who one interacts with. He explained that it is hard to learn the local language when 'not' in contact with its speakers. This also shows that either locals spoke Shona or the outsiders relied on personal networks of outsiders.

Identity card numbers

There were complaints by outsiders that local authority officials used national identity numbers to discriminate against outsiders in the allocation of residential plots. The Zimbabwe national identity card shows the bearer's name; bearer's likeness, sex, district or town of birth and name of chief or village of origin (apparently all blacks, whether urban or rural born have a chief). The most important aspect of the card is the identity number whose first two digits denote the district at which the individual applied for the card and the last two digits denote the 'district of origin' or the father's district of birth (it is always assumed that people are patrilineal in descent[7]). Beitbridge's code is 02. Generally people apply for identity cards at the district offices of their district of origin or in the capital city which is the headquarters of the Registrar General's office. The card also indicates whether or not the holder is a citizen using the letter C for citizen or A for alien. Identity numbers might also be suffixed with the letters 'CIT' for citizens.

Identity cards are needed in business interactions where proof of identity is required[8]. Local authority and government officials deny using identity cards to clandestinely discriminate against people from other districts. Anecdotal reports show that the practice is in fact nationally widespread in civil society organizations; the public and private sectors whether in job applications or in welfare programs. Apparently the district codes[9] enable officials to weed out undeserving applicants. This means that regionalism and nepotism are much more widespread than acknowledged in official circles.

Livelihood strategies as definers of localness

Locals claimed that 'outsiders' brazenly do jobs that locals consider too humiliating to do or are a public acknowledgement of poverty and desperation. This is considered shameful and that it speaks ill of one's social background and upbringing. Vending is one such occupation. It was noted that when children participate in it they are socialised into money too early in life which makes them much harder to control in their teens and beyond as they quickly realize their ability to earn money and become independent of parental control. Locals who are involved in vending are looked at with suspicion as people who have been corrupted culturally or are otherwise desperate. One informant illustrated the point by noting that Venda children do not readily take to vending even when there is a crisis unlike Shona children. He noted that:

> Abantwana besiVendeni ngitsho sekulanjwa njani ngekhaya ungathi bathwale inditshi bayethengisa abavumi ngenxa yokuti abazalelwanga kikho. Kuyabayangisa. Kodwa uzwa umuntu wesiShoneni esithi mina ngafunda ngemali yedobi. ('Venda children do not agree to be sent to sell anything no matter how serious a family crisis is because it is not their way of life. Vending embarrasses them. By contrast among the Shona it is common to hear people saying my school fees came from the sale/vending of peanut butter).

Because of this socialisation into money at an early stage, outsiders were said to be greedy, uncooperative/competitive and aggressive in business. It was said that they do not share information about where they are sourcing goods or information about business in general. Thus 'locals' complain that people 'from the east' love money to a point where they can sell anything and everything including things that should not be sold such as sex as seen in the perceived prominence of outsiders in prostitution. In addition 'locals' said this is why it is more expensive to marry women 'from the east' because their parents literally sell them into marriage. That is women from the east command a high bridewealth. Informants lamented the fact that the high bridewealth should be paid on demand or else the marriage does not take place which they complained is against what they perceived to be the ideals of marriage payments.

Locals claimed that because of this love of money 'outsiders' are notorious for the purchase of goblins/zombies from South Africa for purposes of self-enrichment using clandestine and uncouth supernatural means including witchcraft. Evidence cited for this is the apparent ritualised throwing away of money as part of discarding troublesome goblins/zombies or to cleanse one of bad luck. 'Locals' claimed it was no longer advisable to pick up money in Beitbridge because one might also pick up goblins or bad luck in the process.[10] 'Outsiders' allegedly seek traditional and faith healers' assistance[11] to succeed in business by hurting or otherwise disadvantaging locals.

In order to substantiate arguments about the proliferation of vending as somewhat deviant, improper and wayward, several informants lamented the recent mass commercialisation of marula nuts[12] (Sotho) or mapfura in Shona (from the fruit of sclerocyra birrea) by people from 'the east' as a sign of cultural corruption. The multipurpose sclerocyra birrea tree is characteristic of low lying and semi arid areas in Southern Africa. Its fruit ripens from end of January to mid March. From the fruit women make a seasonal fruit juice or wine when fermented for 48 or 72 hours depending on desired taste and alcohol content. The fruit can also be used as a condiment for traditional vegetables as well as food for goats. The acquisition of the fruit from the wild and juice/wine processing are labour intensive processes involving older women who might be less involved in farming which also takes place at the same time. The stone of the fruit is acquired in the wine/juice making process and allowed to dry for future extraction of nuts in the dry season when people are no longer working in the fields. Alternatively the stones are obtained from goat pens which spit the stones when they chew the cud.

To get the nut, older women crack the stones, one at a time by holding the marula stone steady between two fingers on a stone and hitting with another stone while being careful not to crush one's fingers. The cylindrical, edible white nuts are dislodged carefully using a twig, acacia thorn or anything similar. Locals explained that traditionally old women crack the stones for their grandchildren as part of keeping the children quiet or spoiling them. The nuts are also eaten straight away or boiled and salted lightly as a delicious snack. Again this an activity in which grandmothers are the centre of attention. The nuts can also be pounded into a butter used as a cooking aid in lieu of peanut butter again as a rare treat. Older women could sell marula nuts within their locales or to people they know to buy a few, small personal effects like tea leaves, sugar, soap and so on. Due to the labour intensive nature of cracking the stones to get the nuts, old women usually sell small quantities at a time. By contrast able-bodied 'outsiders' were making brisk business selling bucketfuls of the nuts in Beitbridge. Due to the drought, peanuts were in short supply. These nuts seemed to fill the void. Respondents wondered how one cracks enough of the nut to fill buckets as people from the east seemed able to. Implied here was use of magical powers. 'Locals' saw this, as a sign of greed on the part of 'outsiders'. They did not seem to question their own role as a market in the sale of the nuts.

Locals used words which translate to 'impropriety' (akufanelanga) or that it is 'humiliating'/'embarrassing' (kuyayangisa) to describe the sale of marula nuts. Outsiders countered that locals are 'lazy' and hence they do not take advantage of this nut to make money given a ready market. They wondered why locals buy the nuts from outsiders if their sale is improper. Asked about the ability to fill bucketfuls of this nut they said they bought the cracked nuts from several women crackers in their home villages. Some vendors admitted that they did not know how to crack the nuts and conceded that they could not individually crack enough stones to fill buckets with the nut.

Subsequent to fieldwork in Beitbridge, I discovered that in neighbouring Gwanda district, people also crack the nuts for export to Botswana. There were claims that Tswanas are too lazy to process such delicacies themselves.[13] The cross border traders accumulated bucketfuls by buying small quantities from several female crackers. Thus although people from neighbouring districts whom some respondents in Beitbridge consider locals do not seem involved in the sale of marula nuts in Beitbridge, they are exporting the nut to Botswana a comparatively more lucrative market on account of exchange rates.

Street trade in foreign currency

Due to changes in Zimbabwe's relations with major western donors as a result of land reform, protest over the year 2000's parliamentary election results among other issues, the country experienced crippling foreign currency shortages since the beginning of 2000. Calls for local currency devaluation went unheeded. This led to foreign currency being traded clandestinely in places other than the licensed ones (banks and bureaux de change) to avoid low official exchange rates (1USD:Zim $55 in 2000 and in 1USD: Zim $840 in 2002-3). In the process official markets were starved of the much-needed foreign currency leading to crippling 'shortages' of fuel and other basic commodities on official markets due to hoarding, using goods for speculative purposes in anticipation of local currency losing value at which point the commodities were sold at a high value in the parallel markets. (Parallel market exchange rates at the time of doing fieldwork in 2003 hovered between USD 1: Z$3 000 and 4 000). This intensified economic difficulties in an environment already fraught with hardship.

Foreign currency trade was therefore one of the most lucrative businesses nationwide but especially in Beitbridge because its border post is open 24 hours a day and the high volume of traffic. However the trade locked the country in a vicious circle of high inflation, poverty and increased migration in search of foreign currency. When the country was lumbered with the shortage of local bank notes, illegal trade foreign currency trade was blamed. It was blamed for breakdown of law and order and the proliferation of illegal activities. It has been widely rumoured that the foreign currency traders were fronts many times removed from powerful patrons based in major cities. These patrons supplied their clients with cash as well as protection from harassment by security agents.

In Beitbridge foreign currency trade carried multidimensional risks. From mid 2002,[14] security was tightened in all border posts with undercover operatives (from different security branches) planted everywhere to study the situation with a view to make arrests. Thus some of the people who posed as foreign currency traders or even buyers could have been security operatives. Some participants in this trade were nabbed this way while many others were arrested in numerous crackdowns.

In addition some 'traders' were in fact thieves pretending to be traders or security agents in order to steal from travelers. As noted by FHI (2003) this border post is the Wild West of Southern Africa. Life is fast and one can make and lose money quickly to thieves, commercial sex workers or to security agents. Naturally under such circumstances tension and anxiety are not far from the surface. Thus most traders operate in groups of kin or homegirl/homeboy networks. Competition is stiff. Some have regular clients who are contacted by cellphone which is increasingly an essential tool of the trade. Security risks are increased where foreign currency traders have no bank accounts. (Most do not because one needs a formal sector job with a pay slip; a gross salary of a certain amount; a traceable known address[15] to open a bank account). Thus most foreign currency traders carried money on their person or kept it safe somewhere discrete. With so many people milling around and foreign currency trade taking place in the open it was easy to be pursued by thieves. Besides foreign traders were very distinct; the women carried rather large handbags while men wore cargo trousers (with multiple pockets) used to store the less bulky foreign currency. Some might also carry small backpacks where calculators, cellphones and cash are stored. The multiple pockets are also a risk aversion strategy in the event of mugging.

Foreign currency trade involves illegal border crossings to the South African side of the border, where traders buy rands from people coming to Zimbabwe and sell rands to people going to South Africa on the Zimbabwean side of the border. Male foreign currency traders are generally much more mobile and do business on either side of the border. With so many unlawful activities, risk taking and vulnerabilities associated with street foreign currency trade, arrests were frequent. They were explained in terms of local-outsider relations thereby deepening mutual distrust between the two groups. There were accusations and counter accusations of sneeching, use of witchcraft (goblins/zombies from South Africa) to beat the competition as well use of local fetishes. Citing the presence of a stuntman from Masvingo (a town and province of Shona speaking people) who walks on stilts and sometimes works with some 'fire eaters', locals said this was evidence of outsiders' propensity to use muti (traditional herbs and supernatural forces) because no normal person 'eats fire'. The use of trinkets which people the world over hang in cars on the rearview mirror was another example. Some locals claim that these trinkets are muti which owners pretend is car décor. Outsiders countered that locals are more prone to the use of offensive muti forcing them to seek 'fortification' (defensive muti) to protect themselves and their businesses from accidents, arrests, theft and to counter witchcraft attacks. A consortium of 4 brothers from Mutare involved in foreign currency trade related how they went to their hometown to get fortification. Asked to elaborate on the fortification, they vaguely indicated that among other unspecified things they do not open the trunk where they keep their money in the presence of other people. It sounded like a sensible thing to do given the circumstances. Our informant, the eldest brother was adamant that harm would come the way of anyone who attempted to open the truck without permission. Another man from Chipinge, also admitted using muti as fortification. He owns and drives a taxi. He sought the fortification after surviving what he called 'a near fatal mysterious road accident' which he claimed was because of envious local colleagues in the taxi business. Taxi owners/drivers compete fiercely for people in an environment now invaded by pushcarts. Pushcart owners can push luggage while its owner walks side-by-side with the pushcart at a fraction of the taxi fare.

Male-female relations: disrespectful outsider men or loose local women?

a) The increase in the number of children born out of wedlock

Differences and tensions between locals and outsiders were also expressed in terms of male and female (sexual) liaisons and relationships. Locals blamed outsider males for 'spoiling' local young women and leaving them pregnant without marrying them or paying 'damages' (penalties for seduction[16]) made to the head of patrilineage as compensation for reducing the future marriagability of and bridewealth receipts for lineage daughters thereof. 'Damages' as admission of guilt can also double as a prelude to marriage and the full range of marriage payments (see Ncube 1989:32-4). Local males as fathers feel deprived of bridewealth and disrespected as a result of the perceived waywardness and irresponsibility of outsider males who do not take responsibility for the illicit sex they have with local women. Local men argue that in patrilineal practice it is improper for a man to 'spoil' another man's daughter or sister with impunity. Because 'outsider men' are in Beitbridge on their own without any relatives and some have no fixed abodes, the aggrieved men cannot send their sisters or daughters away to live with the culprits or to force the culprits to take responsibility through shaming and exerting pressure on a wider range of kin. The fathers cannot claim 'damages' in the traditional fashion since this requires a gathering of critical male and female relatives of both parties. Where young women are forced to live with the men they just live together with no traditional rituals to formalise the union. This is considered shameful, as is the only option left, that of allowing the pregnant woman to raise her child while living with her relatives. In reality this is becoming very common. Thus liaisons between local women and outsiders males is a result of and creates multi-layered moral dilemmas. On the one hand a lot of eligible local bachelors as well as married ones are away as migrants. Men migrating into Beitbridge en route to South Africa who might have left their wives back home fill the void left by Beitbridge men. Given their transience they fill the void temporarily although the consequences of such unions (pregnancies) are not so transient. Older people try to discourage local women from dating 'outsider' males but there are few 'local' male alternatives.

Respondents say that 'outsider' men have a lot of money to spend on the young women and promise them marriage and yet they do not marry them. All they want is sex and make no commitment to marriage. Apparently outsider males spoil several local women. This is seen as a sign of moral depravity, insensitivity and provocation of locals by 'outsider' males who prey on local women's naïveté. One got the impression that the naïveté of local women was seen as a virtue.

Local women keenly highlighted their own innocence and naïveté and accused outsider males of being predatory and ruthless. For instance, a 26-year-old woman from Plumtree (a nearby district) recollected the story of her informal marriage with a man 'from the east'. In 2000 she came to Beitbridge with two friends with a view to go to South Africa as illegal immigrants. In typical fashion for people intending to jump the border, they hung around the main bus terminus waiting for nightfall to make their way to the border. They were approached

17

by a young man 'from the east' who offered to assist them with advice. He bought them food. She was overwhelmed by his kindness. By nightfall the young man seemed more interested in convincing the women to stay rather than go to South Africa, saying it was dangerous. She was persuaded. Her friends were not convinced and determined and proceeded to South Africa leaving her behind with the young man. She ended up cohabiting with him. At first the relationship was materially and emotionally satisfactory until she fell pregnant five months later when the relationship turned violent and unpredictable. The man did not come home for several days at a time and money was short forcing her to get an informal sector job. She now has two children with him. To this day they have not performed any traditional rituals to cement the relationship or to formalise it into a traditional marriage. She now suspects that the man has another wife at his rural home 'wherever that is'. She says that men from the east have no respect for the emotions of women from her part of the country. This young lady now deals in foreign currency while trying to raise two children as a single parent. She feels hurt and her hopes of going to South Africa have been dashed. She cannot face her parents with two 'fatherless children'. Another 23-year-old female foreign currency dealer reiterated that women who work in the informal sector are viewed as loose. They have to contend with unsolicited male attention and requests for paid sex. She noted that most women end up with unwanted children. Some of the children are abandoned at Beitbridge Hospital because they are critically ill perhaps due to HIV infection. Many women end up combining paid sex with whatever informal sector activity they engage in because the latter usually has low returns.

'Outsider' males on the other hand accused local women of being 'easy', 'loose' and 'lazy'. They explained that local women do not want to work but prey on working men to make money through sex. The married women are said to be adulterous too when their husbands are away. Another outsider male noted local women do not make ideal wives noting that in his rural Chipinge women work in the fields from sunrise to sunset. He said if he ever married a woman from Beitbridge, she would not cope with peasant life in Chipinge. This would bring ridicule to him. He would rather marry a homegirl who understands his customs and have fun with local women while he is in Beitbridge.

b) Women as border jumpers relying on self-styled male 'travel consultants'

Male-female sexual liaisons also occur in the process of being assisted to cross the border especially when relying on magumaguma. Locals claim magumaguma are 'outsider' males who are easily deported from South Africa because 'Shonas do not speak other people's languages'. We have reason to think that in reality magumaguma are a mixed group of criminal elements from different parts of the country attracted to Beitbridge by the possibility of relatively lucrative criminal activities. (We were unable to interview any self confessed magumaguma to confirm this). Because most magumaguma in Beitbridge are people of no fixed abode and are feared, they cannot ordinarily attract women as partners unless they have causal sex with commercial sex workers. They take advantage of their status as 'travel consultants' for border jumpers and smugglers to abuse women sexually after extracting consultancy fees anticipated or rendered services. Intending border jumpers and smugglers are led into the forest in the dark under the pretext of crossing the border where they might be mugged, raped or forced to consent to sex. Women cannot negotiate for safe sex under these conditions. Some would-be border jumpers are left to their devices in the forest at night where they risk being attacked by wild animals. Some drown in the crocodile infested Limpopo River under unclear circumstances or simply because they cannot swim and do not know which parts of the river to avoid.[17] Women reported that magumaguma make their clients feel insecure and therefore more dependent on them. Those women who are lucky to return to Beitbridge might find themselves pregnant or infected with an STI but relieved of their possessions and money. They cannot report such matters to the police because border jumping is illegal anyway. In addition it is hard to identify offenders because these activities happen at night. The pregnancies might be aborted or the babies abandoned at the hospital later. The humiliation and debasement these women suffer might lead them into commercial sex work to make ends meet rather than go back empty handed. After such humiliation fear of HIV seems rather secondary because such abuse might be the cause of infection.

c) Commercial sex work

'Outsider' women were breaking local marriages through prostitution involving local married men. Local married women lamented that they have known no peace in their marriages since 'these' women descended on Beitbridge. The commercial sex workers are said to use traditional medicines to enhance their sexual performance. Married men disappear for days at a time and return when their wages and salaries are finished. Local married women complained that HIV and AIDS wreaks havoc in Beitbridge as a result of these women yet the government is not doing anything about it. Married women called for the ban of 'shebeens'.[18] Men were a little conciliatory claiming that visiting commercial sex workers was 'now a way of life'. There is very little they could do about it. Some men indicated that when wives are not around they have no choice but to visit commercial sex workers.

The majority of commercial sex workers we interviewed admitted being from other parts of Zimbabwe including Matabeleland region making them locals if one uses the foregoing criteria. Some of the women originally came to Beitbridge with the intention of going to South Africa but got stuck in Beitbridge and resorted to prostitution to make ends meet; some were attracted to Beitbridge by what was perceived as a good opportunity to practice commercial sex work on account of an increase in travelers and truck drivers while others are locals pushed into commercial sex work by lack of viable alternative employment. Some tried working as domestics and gave up when they realized how little they earned. Whatever their initial intention, commercial sex workers said theirs is one of the most lucrative income generating activities in Beitbridge. Business was described as brisk leading to some women taking cannabis to maintain their stamina because of high demand for their services.

The women define prostitution as real work. Although some readily accept that they are commercial sex workers others like Debbie, 25 years old, does not like the term. She sees herself as a worker doing more strenuous work than most people. Thandi, 32 years and from Bulawayo (within the same province in which Beitbridge is found) the owner of a shebeen looks at herself as a businesswoman who has to make sure that her clients are happy and that the fridges are well stocked with alcoholic drinks. Asked about risks of HIV infection given its high prevalence and the institutionalisation of premium fees for condomless sex, Rati a 27-year-old commercial sex worker said there are 'risks' and 'occupational hazards' in any occupation.

'Locals' said 'outsiders' are involved in commercial sex work because they have no relatives in town to be ashamed of. Thus commercial sex workers who were born and raised in Beitbridge generally try to be discreet by meeting clients away from home in bars, in trucks and at night while outsiders can bring men to rented houses any time of day. Outsiders can also apparently brazenly run shebeen with 'rest rooms' (that is, bedrooms in which clients can also meet commercial sex workers)..

Fees for sex were rated as 'short time' or a full night; with or without a condom. At the time of doing research women charged Z$3 000 per short time on a take-it or leave-it basis and Z$20 000 without condoms for a full night. That is, 1USD for a short time or 6USD for condomless sex if one uses prevailing parallel market exchange rates of 1 USD: Z$3 000). Others say that the reason why condomless sex is expensive is to cater for risks and to discriminate between those who are really determined and those not so prepared to take the risks.

When demand is high some of the commercial sex workers say they smoke cannabis which gives them more stamina. They see 10 or more men in 24 hours depending on one's energy levels and demand. They define theirs as real work and not pleasure.

Mavis, 26 years old and a local, confessed to being a commercial sex worker. She operates a market stall in the afternoon and sees clients in the night. She pointed out that paid sex is more lucrative than the returns from the stall. Earnings from paid sex are highest when one is paid in South African currency which is later sold on the parallel market. She claims that married women with 'negligent' husbands are increasingly resorting to paid sex with strangers or regular clients. 'Negligent' husbands engage in adulterous relationships and are unable to meet family needs such as food, accommodation, good clothes, toiletries and pocket money because they give their earnings to other women. She asked rhetorically why should women sit at home when they cannot feed the children? Her husband was in prison after being involved in a near fatal fist fight. She said she would stop having paid sex with other men when her husband returned. Other than personal upkeep other women who engage in commercial sex work also remit money to their parents and children. Relatives are not told what the source of the income is.

Shortage of Accommodation and the Increase in Crime

As indicated above, in the 1990s accommodation was already in short supply in Beitbridge. Due to the influx of people it has now reached crisis proportions. Lodgers call friends and relatives to share the small huts. In 2002 one could find four women sharing a small hut. The overcrowding and the anonymity of baghdads have further given credence to the idea that outsiders 'brought problems to Beitbridge'. The deviant activities of users of baghdads have stigmatised the settlement.

In 2002 in preparation for the second solar eclipse on 4 December 2002, the town council destroyed the baghdads because they were considered an eyesore for tourists who were expected to visit Zimbabwe. This led to a worse accommodation problem in Beitbridge. Most bona fide owners of the plots with baghdads lamented the escalating cost of building materials saying they are no longer able to build houses which meet stipulated town standards. With the destruction of baghdads they have lost a steady source of income.

Consequently parallel to US plans to pulverise the Iraqi capital, Baghdad to force a regime change, Beitbridge was also planning to destroy its 'Baghdad' as part of a clean up operation ironically codenamed 'Operation Baghdad must go' to flush out deviants and the embarrassing dwellings they used. After the demolition of the baghdads, inhabitants relocated to start an informal settlement by the rubbish dump a place called 'Emara' in Ndebele (literally this means 'at the rubbish dump'). This has also become home for some of the worst and as yet unapprehended criminals in Beitbridge. Because the place is hidden from view because of the cover of trees, the town authorities have not interfered with the residents of this settlement. It has its own informal market place 'by the river' (emfuleni) where illegal activities take place: gambling, the sale of stolen property and so on. Security is non-existent. Locals claim that the residents of Emara are outsiders with no accommodation in the town. They are incensed that town authorities have not punished these outsiders for establishing a settlement in an illegal place. They complained town authorities harassed and dispossessed owners of baghdads, who are locals leaving them with no income yet their shacks were on officially allocated plots. Locals complained that residents of Emara steal and slaughter locals' livestock which wonder to the area from nearby rural areas. After slaughter they take only the legs and leave the rest of the carcass to rot. Locals say that outsiders are 'not cattle people' and hence they kill animals with such brutality and only for a few kilograms of meat. Some of the animals they steal are allegedly ferried to Masvingo (a neighbouring province) for sale making it hard for investigators to make timely follow-ups. At the time of doing fieldwork there were no arrests of cattle rustlers from this area. Because this informal settlement offers anonymity to thieves and seemed to embrace outsi-ders at the expense of locals, the latter wanted it destroyed.

In spite of Emara, there are many homeless people with nowhere to sleep at night particularly the recently deported, other unemployed people and travelers in transit. They loiter all night for safety or try to sleep inside pubs where they are likely to be chased away when the bars close. Some of the nocturnal movements are encouraged by the border which is open 24 hours. Foreign currency changers might prefer to do business at night although it is very risky for all involved. However, some of these night movements may be attributed to criminals. A local male lamented that '... "outsiders" find the night too long that they do not sleep when others do. They use the cover of dark to make more money through theft'.

Because of the increase in crime, locals were reluctant to give outsider males accommodation if they are not of a known profession or known former address within Beitbridge. Locals related personal stories or those of relatives and neighbours who were victims or nearly victims of theft by a lodger. The four brothers from Mutare referred to earlier also attested to this. The eldest brother who came to Beitbridge in 1999 says that it was easier then to get accommodation in baghdads but now it was impossible because of the increase in crime. Outsiders are suspected of engaging in crime but he said not all outsiders are criminals; it is only desperate recently deported border jumpers who engage in criminal activities.

Consequently some 'outsider' informal sector traders sleep in the open on rock outcrops on which they do business. They do their ablutions in the open under cover of darkness which locals say is indecent and unhygienic. Most outsiders and locals concur that defecating and urinating in the open or under bushes is a recipe for a public health crisis. Beitbridge had a cholera outbreak in the late 1990s. People were fearful that in the rainy season the likelihood of another cholera outbreak was very likely. Thus outsiders' activities are seen a public health threat. In addition there were complaints by locals that homeless outsiders were vandalizing town property and facilities such as public toilets rendering them unusable. Outsiders were accused of having no 'commitment' to Beitbridge or civic pride and hence their vandalism.

Other respondents (locals and outsiders) also concurred that there is a problem of people who roam the town at night for purposes of theft and wanted something done about it. In the past people could leave clothes outside on the washing line over night, leave windows open overnight on account of the stifling heat or doors unlocked while running an errand all of which is no longer possible. Instead one needs burglar bars to deter house break-ins through windows. It was highlighted with regret that mobility at night is no longer advisable unless one is armed or in the company of others. Otherwise one risks muggings, assault and/or death. Locals accused the police of inaction. Some informants accused the police of receiving bribes from people 'from the east' who are allegedly awash with money obtained through illegal means. Otherwise why are they unable to catch the thieves in such a small town with very few hiding places, they asked rhetorically?

Some locals accused outsiders of corruption which enabled them to access residential plots ahead of locals. One 'local' 26 year old female lodger renting from an 'outsider' was particularly angry and wondered how the outsider got the land and the house ahead of her. She said 'outsiders' brought problems to Beitbridge including accommodation shortages. She said: 'I have no accommodation in my own town and none in other towns. It is not fair'.

Outsiders allege that locals do not appreciate the value of immovable property. They prefer to have cash to land. Consequently they sell their plots if they have a cashflow crisis. A man in his 60s from Chipinge observed that it was easy to get a stand sold by a local. He was of the opinion that there was no need to deal with the local authority when one wants a residential plot. The local authority demands the impossible and tends to scrutinise identity cards. It is better to deal with desperate locals. Although he came to Beitbridge in 1999 he bought a plot and built a six-roomed house in which he lives. He has two lodgers. He has bought a second plot from a local. He has since relocated his children to Beitbridge and he sees Beitbridge as a place full of opportunities by virtue of its proximity to South Africa. He sells car spares and he is happy with his business. He said locals are 'lazy' and 'lack competence' in business and should not label others as 'outsiders' if they are Zimbabweans. Other than crime which he said is on the increase, his other complaint is the weather which is too hot for business especially when one is moving on foot from place to place.

Discussion

The foregoing clearly shows that respondents who define themselves as 'locals' see themselves as more entitled to resources and opportunities associated with Beitbridge's as a social, political and administrative space while 'outsiders' counter this in many ways often challenging criteria locals use to claim entitlements. Thus issues at stake are identities, belonging and entitlement; to whom should Beitbridge's resources go? From the foregoing people have a notion of who belongs, why and how even though these notions are contested and contestable on many fronts (see Cesarani and Fulbrook 1996). Differences of meanings and criteria of who belongs, when and how exist between indigenes and immigrants (Assiter 1999). This is why some of the criteria given are contradictory.

In literature it has been noted that belonging is about real and imagined connections between people and 'their' physical space/territory (Assiter 1999; Alund 1999). Some scholars have elaborated that genealogical connections are considered critical in determining belonging (see Harnishfeger 2004; Geshiere 2001, Assiter 1999) but also a common history, language and culture. Thus respondents in this study made reference to clan names, common chieftaincies, rural backgrounds and languages as indicators of localness. However the latter criterion also includes people from the wider Matabeleland region whose culture is considerably different from that of Vendas and Shanganis but are considered locals by virtue of historical legacies. In the colonial era the country was divided into two administrative regions Mashonaland apparently for Shona speaking peoples and Matabeleland for Ndebele speaking people (see Worby 1994; CCJP 1997). After independence, the infamous Matabeleland atrocities also used this broad categorisation to 'discipline' 'Ndebeles' then understood to be anti-government and anti-Shona. The latter were at the helm. This deepened a sense of 'us' and 'them' whose seeds were sown in the colonial era. In reality Matabeleland is, or 'Ndebeles' are a collection of diverse cultural and language groups including Venda, Shangani, Sotho, Kalanga, Tonga, Nambya, the Khoi San and so on. Historically some of these groups nursed differences albeit subjected to Ndebele dominance in the Ndebele kingdom. Because in popular representation all these diverse cultural groups are still defined as Ndebele as a result of the interplay of historical factors and geography, respondents in this study seemed to view members of these language groups as 'locals' too. However there are indications that the inability to master Venda by some 'locals' annoyed some Venda respondents who despise the fact that their language and culture is not considered important enough to learn. They resent the fact that some people can carry their culture and language with them wherever they are going while their language and culture does not have an imprint on visitors even within their own town and distinct. Thus although people 'from the east' seem easy to single out as outsiders, complaints raised against them also apply to some locals. There is evidence that Ndebele speaking women who marry Venda speaking men also do not learn local languages effectively contributing to the extinction of the local language. Thus localness also seems graduated and not as clear-cut as it seems at face value. Concerns about the future of local languages expresses an anxiety about the impact of 'outsider' languages on local culture. This anxiety is pervasive throughout discussions of localness which points to the fragility of identities (Kellner 1992) and interlocutors' need to preserve them.

These issues are made more complex by national registration numbers which for administrative purposes encode districts into identity cards. Districts themselves have over the years been encoded as belonging to specific ethnic and language groups thanks to colonial 'ethnocartography' (Worby 1994) whose imprint has endured to this day. Thus given decentralisation in which districts are supposed to administer limited resources to develop areas under their jurisdiction, undertones of ethnocartography seem to determine who/which ethnic group belongs in which district and therefore is entitled to resources of that district. In this vein ethnicity easily becomes a marker of who belongs in which district. This is aided by national identity cards which detail chiefs and so on. The identity card is therefore not just about Zimbabwean citizenship per se; it denotes district and village citizenship for black Zimbabweans.[19] It therefore provides a formal and seemingly indisputable means of covertly excluding others. Consequently migrants are officially encoded as invaders/ outsiders in other districts. In the face of limited and shrinking resources and opportunities at district level indigenes are assumed to have preferential entitlement to local resources (see Nyambara 2001; Hammar 2001) while in some cases where the migrants come from dominant groups they are able to mobilise networks of powerful compatriots to consolidate their dominance and deepen the marginalisation of locals who are ethnic minorities at the national level (see Dzingirai 1996; Harnischfeger 2004; Madzudzo and Dzingirai 1995). As noted by Nyamnjoh (2002) within nations there are gradations of and qualifications to entitlements so that some groups are construed as less entitled than others in general or in certain circumstances. In other words, in people's lived realities the social exclusion of some groups is necessary if the interlocutors' entitlements are to be guaranteed. Because of the persistence of tension over what can be said about ethnic differences especially those involving the Shona-Ndebele divide as popularly defined (Worby 1994; Dzingirai 1996), tensions between locals and outsiders are expressed in other means such as complaints about the environment, public health and so on. Direct reference to ethnicity is avoided as is challenging the prevailing status quo.

Thus as noted by Comaroff and Comaroff (2001), belonging is also about membership in a material and moral community. Boundaries of these communities are marked by more than objective markers of identity card numbers and physical boundaries between provinces and districts, they are nuanced in local culture and language. The salience of outsider languages is seen as a signal of the presence of outsiders who have resisted assimilation and are thus rejected for insisting to stand out rather than assimilate (see Bauman 1997). Assimilation of course is about obliterating differences and acquiescing to the dominance of local culture. Failure to assimilate challenges local culture and hence the hysteria against it.

The incessant complaints about outsiders' lack of civic pride, their being harbingers of HIV and AIDS, crime, prostitution, accommodation shortages, and broken marriages should be seen as hysteria over the transgression of the boundaries of moral and material communities in a context where opportunities and material resources are shrinking (Comaroff and Comaroff 2001). Boundaries define those who are entitled and those who are not. The influx of migrants in an already impoverished area such as Beitbridge gives its residents a sense of being overrun, beaten to the high table in their own backyards, being squeezed out of their territory. Thus what one might define as xenophobia is about redefining 'us' against 'them' and therefore defining who is invited to the high table as a guest and who should be a servant serving the guests lest the food runs out if too many people come as guests (see Nyamnjoh 2004). The outcry over degradation and 'problems' brought by migrants is really moral panic (Comaroff and Comaroff 2001). Ungar (2001) defines moral panic as a public concern connected to perceived social deviance or crises which threaten life as people idealise it.

Usually moral panic relies on exaggeration of threats and raises 'issue attention cycles' when people focus on a particular issue over a long period. Usually the issue is debated as some kind of impending disaster. In the case of Beitbridge the disaster(s) was/were connected to health issues (the upsurge in HIV and AIDS, the threat of cholera due to filth), security (inability to walk across town at night, theft) and social decay seen in the increase in the number of women raising children out of wedlock and the increase in adultery in general. Moral panic creates a sense of consensus and simplifies an otherwise complex reality. Outsiders become soft targets (see Gray 1998) to whom all problems and anxieties are attributable. The consensus enables people not to look at their own roles in the situation they are complaining about. In the case of Beitbridge the consensus is that outsiders are the bearers of all problems that bedevil the small town. This neither critiques the local authority's administrative style especially its failure to comprehensively increase housing stock, to collect refuse and provide sanitation befitting an urban area nor central government's inability to come to its aid and to ensure effective policing of the town.

While admitting that the 'us' against 'them' ethos predates economic reform, its manifestation under the latter should also be seen as a sign of 'disintegration' in the wake of the contradictory developments spawned by the neoliberal dispensation (Friedman 1997). Friedman (1997) notes that at the impoverished margins conflict over resources is particularly stiff as livelihoods are turfed and territorialised. He defines xenophobia as 'ethnification' or ethnicised turfing/closure of resources. It affects the poor and less educated more than elites whose livelihoods are de-territorialised as they move to the diaspora to make ends meet on account of their skills (Friedman 1997:84). For the poor xenophobia is a form of self-preservation in the face of real or imagined threats (Friedman 1997).

Thus xenophobia is connected to livelihoods at the margin where the turf is not just in the material world but also in the moral community as a source of solace from being battered and humiliated in the former. Thus control over women and children become important and hence the outrage local women's sexuality (see Moghadam 1994). Local men see local women's relations with outsider males as an affront to their identities because outsider males do not give local males their patrilineal dues. On the other hand outsider women who marry local men deny them the full range of patrilineal respect by not learning local languages making their children unable to speak it too. In this vein outsiders are considered disrespectful to locals' moral community.

Tensions over 'proper' male and female behaviour have to be connected to migration as a livelihood strategy. Historically men migrated internally and internationally to acquire resources to establish independent households and to maintain them. In Beitbridge and neighbouring districts men went to South Africa. However they are no longer welcome there. Thus deportations have rendered quests to prove one's masculinity on the labour market rather 'perilous' as Kimmel (1998) observes. The resulting inability to meet family needs leads to affected males being incommunicado with their wives and children back home. As noted by Chikovore *et al.* (2002) is some cases it leads to violence against wives or girlfriends when the men come home on that occasional visit. However migration also becomes a diplomatic exit option for those young men who are not ready to marry but are under pressure to do so because a girlfriend is pregnant. It is hard to stay in the same area with a girl one has made pregnant without marrying her. It creates tension between families of the young man and woman. Some young men in this predicament may be the ones who are stuck in Beitbridge, they cannot go to South Africa on account of repeated deportations but cannot go back home on account of unresolved matters there. They stay in Beitbridge to ponder their next move and to try and raise enough income for one's sustenance and for remittances back home.

Such young men are likely get emotional attachment and affection through temporary relations with local women some of whom end up pregnant and are pressurised by male kin to marry the men responsible who invariably are not forthcoming. Some cohabit with the women which riles male kin of the latter (see also Stitcher 1995; Barnes and Win 1992). It would not make sense under such circumstances to go back home with another pregnant girlfriend when another set of parents is already waiting for bridewealth. Thus most young men live life running away from parental responsibility on account of not having the wherewithal to be parents and husbands. Being trapped in Beitbridge raises more difficulties creating men who are rolling stones, with no homes, no families and unable to sustain either. This stigmatises the men and their female partners. The foregoing shows that beyond the differences between locals and outsiders there is a parallel deepening 'crisis in gender relations' (see Connell 1998). Chant (2000) describes it more as a 'crisis of masculinity'. That is, although people still hold on to ideals of male and female behaviour and relations, they have to deal with a global socio-economic environment which makes it impossible for men especially to get material resources which go with their roles.

For women, lack of education, professional qualifications and/or skills renders meaningful employment impossible. Whereas previously marriage sufficed as a source of security, it is no longer enough on account of low employment opportunities on the part of men. Women too have to seek wage employment. Although some engage in informal sector activities, returns are so

28

low that one cannot take care of oneself let alone raise a family on them. Female migration has been on the increase on account of gaps in male-female relations as described above. Difficulties of crossing the border illegally and repeated deportations lead to paid sex being the only comparatively lucrative alternative in the short term. However migration per se tends to stigmatise women as they move away from families and are seen as out of control (see Barnes 1992; Jeater 1993). The added problem of the proliferation of HIV and AIDS in Beitbridge (prevalences hovering around 50 per cent) leads to migrant women being accused of spreading it. The salience of HIV and AIDS since the 1990s coincides with increased mobility and the human influx into Beitbridge. Outsiders are blamed for it. HIV and AIDS programs are shunned as 'outsider' programs dealing with problems of outsiders. Locals often say 'go and tell those people about HIV and AIDS' (fieldnotes October 2002).

It is also clear from the foregoing that faced with generalised poverty and despair people adopt livelihood strategies that rely on interpersonal relations but underlined by the 'withdrawal-at-will' ethos (see Bauman 1997); a worthy tribute to market reforms perhaps. The relationships are temporary and dependent on market conditions. Time, speed and returns are very important in contracting and terminating relations. Bauman (1997) says that in these relations '...the other [is cast] as the potential source of pleasurable experience...'. Nyamnjoh (2004) explains this as a process of 'mutual zombification' or mutual exploitation and abuse. Consequently although locals accuse outsider males of exploitation, local women exploit them for money; both parties risk contracting HIV in the process. It's a zero sum game. Such predatory relations unfortunately also limit the possibility of solidarity and the extent to which poor people can mobilise to challenge greater forces and institutions that uphold and reproduce their poverty. Senses of community also weaken because of the cash nexus; individuals are concerned only with those pursuits that will ensure that they have food on the table in the immediate future (Melucci 1997). Relations one contracts can bring food or misfortune.

When one looks at informal sector activities such as vending and foreign currency trade, accusation and counter accusations of ill-intent not only point to the importance of social relations for survival but also anxieties associated with these relations. Poverty and stiff competition make it impossible for vendors to share information on livelihoods. The need to get ahead of the competition and what looks like the pathological love for money are seen as deviant and immoral. Locally poverty is seen as shameful. However it seems that it is more what one does with one's poverty which is more embarrassing. In this regard informal sector activities are seen as an embarrassing attempt at resolving this poverty. For men especially when wives participate in informal sector activities it is considered an indictment of one's masculinity. It says he is incapable of looking after his family. These views also point to the fact that the proliferation of vending is relatively new in Beitbridge. Beitbridge residents do not appreciate this change particularly the fact that it is also sucking children into commercial sex work in large numbers. It also points to a different approach and experience to market insertion. For instance, peasant agriculture in Beitbridge revolves around livestock production so that when there is a family a beast or several beasts are sold. However livestock is generally a male domain. This enabled men to be breadwinners without forcing women on the streets. However due to the vagaries of nature (droughts and floods in recent years), livestock production has been disrupted. With migration to South Africa now difficult, women are forced to find means and ways of making ends meet. This is why local women who are vendors are seen and culturally corrupt, more so because some women combine vending with commercial sex work.

Even though locals have a problem with the proliferation of informal sector activities which they see as signs of wanton greed and cultural corruption, they resent the fact that outsiders not only dominate in it but also that they do not disclose their business deals. Locals would rather benefit from their own environment's opportunities even though this 'love for money' is rather new. Thus the need to defend the local turf for locals on the part of locals and the need to carve niches in this strange turf for outsiders leads to tension between locals and outsiders. However the tensions and insecurities of the situation brought about by security agents and thieves is ground for witchcraft accusations as an explanation for failure and personal inability to cope with the situation and a way of discrediting those that look like they are somehow coping with the situation (see also Fisiy and Geshiere 1996 on Cameroon; Niehaus 1993 for Limpopo province in South Africa, Auslander 1993 and Schlyter 1999 for Zambia). Sometimes these accusations make people to rationalise the exclusion of marginalised people by blaming them for prevailing misfortunes. In this vein no one sympathises with recently deported outsiders who are genuinely desperate. Through these accusations and counter accusations, competitors are discredited as immoral, greedy people who subvert the social and moral fabric. Thus in Beitbridge survival strategies of the otherwise very desperate outsiders are seen as a threat to the social fabric as inter-personal relations; they are the source of adultery, the cause children born out of wedlock; lack of security as seen in nocturnal business activities and crime. The benefits that accrue to locals are not admitted since those locals who have latched on this bandwagon are also discredited as culturally corrupted.

Conclusion

Because witchcraft accusations rarely occur in people who do not interact intimately with each other, one can conclude that they point to increased interaction between locals and outsiders under competitive as opposed to cooperative conditions. Thus the emergence of outsider — local consciousness points to (real or imagined) shortage of resources and therefore increased competition. In the case of Beitbridge, and Zimbabwe as a whole the 'shortage' of resources has to be understood within the austerities of neoliberal economic reform which has seen the state rolling back its service provision role leaving a vacuum which donors and other non-state players have not filled. Because there is a call for local authorities to rely on local resources this creates problems where there are people migrating from other parts of the country because they are seen as intruders. Relations of cooperation break down in the competition yielding to predatory relations. Due to the joint effect of neoliberalism and decentralisation local authorities are battling to stretch limited resources to fulfill their mandates for 'local development' but have to contend with an influx of people from other regions running away from the poverty of their regions. Thus outsider-local relations emerge as a way of redefining who gets the limited resources. One can conclude then that this is part of the many contradictions of globalisation where opening up of some spaces seems to go with the closure of others. The poverty unleashed by globalisation threatens existing communities and certainties while the emphasis on market relations and transience of social relations challenges the emergence of new communities (see Alund 1999; Cesarani and Fulbrook 1996; Friedman 1997). A more long-term study is therefore necessary to trace changes in definitions of belonging in a town such as Beitbridge.

Notes

1. The use of race as an indicator of being an indigene has been challenged in the media since many black Zimbabweans trace their roots to other parts of Africa. In other words they are immigrants genealogically just like their white counterparts.

2. Invariably, buses that leave Harare in the morning get to Beitbridge after dark. Those that leave Harare in the evening get there at dawn.

3. While Beitbridge's informal settlement dwellings are truly appalling, I do not think they are 'the worst' per se. They are comparable to dwellings in many other informal settlements all over the country. The difference is that in Beitbridge the informal settlement is in full view of all while in other towns such settlements are somewhat hidden.

4. This term emerged in 1991 during Operation Desert Storm in which pro-west media images of Iraq's capital, Baghdad in the aftermath of bombings showed dilapidated houses and people desperate for basic social amenities. The term is locally used to capture squalor and lack of amenities. It is in fact used to refer to informal settlements in other border towns in Zimbabwen as well.

5. These have ranged from proof of marriage for women (marriage certificates), proof of residence while in South Africa, a faxed invitation from South Africa, proof of employment in Zimbabwe supported by a letter from the employer saying that the applicant is on leave and WILL come back to Zimbabwe after the visit to South Africa, proof of funds in a Zimbabwean bank, proof of possession of South African currency in the form of travelers' cheques issued by a commercial bank in Zimbabwe and so on.

6. This was meant to pre-empt the possibility of suspicion that we were opposition party activists or some other such threat to the nation; a likely accusation given the prevailing political environment.

7. The imposition of patrilineal identities is detrimental for female divorcees and unwary single women with children. It becomes difficult for the women to get documents like birth certificates, national identity cards, passports for their children without tacit approval of the children's fathers. Patrilineal imposition begins with routine antenatal registration where women are asked details of their partners which are subsequently used to confer identities to children.

8. It used to be compulsory to carry a national identity card everywhere because it was an offense to be found without one.

9. Some people indicate their identity numbers on their CVs.

10. During fieldwork I noticed that discarded small denomination of notes were quite prominent in Beitbridge than in Harare where I live. This might be an indication of how worthless these low denominations are.

11. There has been a proliferation of outsider faith and traditional healers in Beitbridge. They treat people of illnesses including those related to HIV and AIDS but also give fortifications and fetishes for a variety of things.

12. The name marula is Sotho. It is used here to make the link between the fruit and the upmarket chocolate cream liqueur called 'Amarula' which is purportedly made from this 'African fruit'.

13. In addition to these nuts Zimbabwean also export dried traditional vegetables, caterpillars of the mopane tree, traditional beans among other traditional goodies.

14 .Since the beginning of 2004, there have been wide ranging anticorruption reforms which have seen foreign currency parallel markets curbed after the introduction of a central bank controlled foreign currency auction system.

15. Usually it is difficult to open an account in one town and give the address of another town. However after the account is opened it is easy to operate it from any part of the country.

16. Pre- and extramarital sex is assumed to be a result of the man seducing the woman especially if the latter is young and presumed sexually naïve.

17. People who die in this way are likely to be buried by the state as 'paupers' through the department of social welfare. Paupers' burials are without ceremony. They apply to people who die without their identity cards and are not claimed by their kin leading to corpses staying in the mortuary for 3 months or longer depending on whether the mortuary can afford to keep the body for that long. We spoke to mortuary officials whose records indicate that lately paupers' burials are on the increase in Beitbridge. They increased from 5 in 1999, to 10 per year in 2000 and 2001, 70 in 2002 and 58 by September 2003 when we were in the field.

18. These are informal sector drinking taverns usually in people's homes. They also double as local brothels in which beer and paid sex are available around the clock. Commercial sex workers contracted to the tavern and not necessarily by the house owner or her family provide the paid sex.

19. The idea that all Africans have chiefs is a colonial creation, which has persisted. It is an anomaly especially for urban-based people. In addition, chiefs' areas of jurisdiction change, people migrate yet issues of 'origin' are inherited from one's father regardless of one's current circumstances. Whites and bi-racial people apparently do not have chiefs and villages encoded on their identity cards.

References

Alund, A., 1999, 'Feminism, Multiculturalism and Essentialism', in Yuval-Davies, N. and Werbner, P., eds., *Women, Citizenship and Difference*, London: Zed Books.

Assiter, A, 1999,'Citizenship Revisited', in Yuval-Davis, N and Werbner, P., eds., *Women, Citizenship and Difference*, London: Zed Books, pp 41-53.

Auslander, M., 1993, 'Open the Wombs!': The Symbolic Politics of Modern Ngoni Witchfinding', in Comaroff, J. and Comaroff, J., eds., *Modernity and its Malcontents: Ritual and Power in Postcolonial Africa*, Illinois: Chicago University Press.

Barnes, T. and Win, E., 1992, *To Live a Better Life*, Harare: Baobab Books.

Barnes, T., 1992, 'The Fight for the Control of African Women's Mobility in Colonial Zimbabwe, 1900-1939', in *Signs*, Vol. 17, No. 3, pp586-608.

Bauman, Z.,1997, 'The Making and Unmaking of Strangers', in Werbner, P. and Modood, T., eds., *Debating Cultural Hybridity: Multicultural Identities and the Politics of Anti-racism*, London: Zed Books.

CCJP, 1997, Breaking the Silence and Building True Peace: A Report on the Disturbances in Matabeleland and Midlands 1980 to 1988, Harare: CCJP/ Legal Resources Foundation.

Cesarani, D. and Fulbrook, M., 1996, 'Introduction', in Cesarani, D. and Fulbrook, M., eds., *Citizenship, Nationality and Migration in Europe*, London: Routledge, pp1-14.

Chant, S., 2000, 'Men in Crisis? Reflection on Masculinity, Work and Family in North West Costa Rica', in *The European Journal of Development Research*, Vol. 12, No. 2.

Chikovore, J. et al., 2002, 'Denial and Violence: Paradoxes in Men's Perspectives to Premarital Sex and Pregnancy in Rural Zimbabwe', Umea University, Sweden.

Comaroff, J., and J., 2001, 'Nurturing the Nation: Aliens, Apocalypse and the Post-colonial State', in *Social Identities*, Vol. 7, No. 2, pp233-265.

Connell, R. W., 1998, 'Masculinities and Globalisation', in *Men and Masculinities*, Vol. 1, No. 1.

Dzingirai, V., 1996, 'Every Man Must Resettle Where he Wants': The Politics of Settlement in the Context of Community Wildlife Management Programme in Binga, Zimbabwe', in *Zambezia*, Vol. 23, No 1.

Fisiy, C. and Geshiere, P., 1996, 'Witchcraft, Violence and Identity: Different Trajectories in Post-colonial Cameroon', in Werbner, R and Ranger, T., eds., *Postcolonial Identities in Africa*, London: Zed Books.

Friedman, J., 1996,'Being in the World: Globalisation and Localization', in Featherstone, M., ed., *Global Culture*, London: Sage Publications.

Friedman, J., 1997, 'Global Crises, the Struggle for Cultural Identity and Intellectual Porkbarrelling: Cosmopolitans versus Locals, Ethnics and Nationals in an Era of De-hegemonisation', in Werbner, P. and Modood, T., eds., *Debating Cultural Hybridity: Multicultural Identities and the Politics of Anti-racism*, London: Zed Books.

FHI, 2003, *Corridors of Hope*, www.fhi.org (accessed in October 2003).

Geshiere, P., 2001, 'Liberalisation, Belonging and the Village in Africa', in Andersson, J. and Breusers, M., eds., *Kinship Structures and Enterprising Actors: Anthropological Essays on Development*, The Netherlands: Wageningen University.

Gaidzanwa, R. B., 'Voting with their Feet: Migrant Zimbabwean Nurses and Doctors in the Era of Structural Adjustment', Uppsala: Nordiska Afrikainstutet.

Gray, C., 1998, 'Cultivating Citizenship through Xenophobia in Gabon, 1960-1995', in *Africa Today*, Vol. 45, No.3-4, pp389-410.

Hammar, A., 2001, 'The Day of Burning': Eviction and Reinvention in the Margins of Northwest Zimbabwe', in *Journal of Agrarian Change*, Vol. 1, No.4, pp550-574.

Harnischfeger, J., 2004, 'Sharia and Control over Territory: Conflict Between 'Settlers' and 'Indigenes' in Nigeria', in *African Affairs*, Vol. 103, pp143-52.

Jeater, D.,1993, *Marriage, Perversion and Power: The Construction of Moral Discourses in Southern Rhodesia, 1894-1930*, Oxford: Clarendon Press.

Kellner, D., 1992, 'Popular Culture and the Construction of Postmodern Identities', in Lash, S. and Friedman, J., eds., *Modernity and Identity*, Oxford UK and Cambridge USA: Blackwell Publishers, pp 141-177.

Kimmel, M. S., 1998, 'Patriarchy's Second Coming as Masculine Renewal', in Claussen, D. S., ed., *Standing on the Promise: Promise Keepers and the Revival of Manhood*, Ohio, The Pilgrim Press.

Lister, R., 1997, *Citizenship: Feminist Perspectives*, London: Macmillan.

Madzudzo, E. and Dzingirai, V., 1995, 'A Comparative Study of the Implications of Ethnicity on CAMPFIRE in Bulilimamangwe and Binga, Zimbabwe', in *Zambezia*, Vol. 22, No 1, pp 25-42.

Melucci, A., 1997, 'Identity and Difference in a Globalized World', in Werbner, P. and Modood, T., eds., *Debating Cultural Hybridity: Multicultural Identities and the Politics of Anti-racism*, London: Zed Books.

Moghadam, V.,1994, 'Introduction: Women and Identity Politics in Theoretical and Comparative Perspective', in Moghadam, V., eds., *Identity, Politics and Women: Cultural Reassertion of Feminisms in International Perspective*, Westview Press.

Ncube, W., 1989, *Family Law in Zimbabwe*, Harare: Legal Resources Foundation,.

Niehaus, I. A.,1993, 'Witchhunting and Political Legitimacy: Continuity and Change in Green Valley, Lebowa, 1939-91', in *Africa*, Vol. 63, No.1.

Nyambara, P., 2001, 'The Closing Frontier: Agrarian Change, Immigrants and the 'Squatter Menace' in Gokwe, 1980-1990s', in *Journal of Agrarian Change*, Vol. 1 No. 4, pp534-549.

Nyamnjoh, F.B., 2002, 'Local Attitudes Towards Citizenship and Foreigners in Botswana: An Appraisal of Recent Press Stories', in *Journal of Southern African Studies*, Vol. 28, No. 4, pp 754-775.

Nyamnjoh, F.B., 2004, 'Globalisation and Popular Disenchantment in Africa', in Mbaku, J.M. and Saxena, S.C., eds., *Africa at the Crossroads: Between Regionalism and Globalisation*, Westport, Connecticut: Praeger.

Nyamnjoh, F.B., Durham, D., and Fokwang, J., 2002, 'The Domestication of Hair and Modernized Consciousness in Cameroon: A Critique in the Context of Globalisation', in *Identity, Culture and Politics: An Afro Asian Dialogue*, Vol. 3, No. 2, pp 98-124.

Pettman, J. J., 1999, 'Globalisation and the Gendered Politics of Citizenship', in Yuval-Davis, N. and Werbner, P., eds., *Women, Citizenship and Difference*, London: Zed Books, pp 207-220.

Potts, D., 1999,'The Impact of Structural Adjustment on Welfare and Livelihoods: An Assessment by the People in Harare, Zimbabwe', in Jones, S. and Nelson, N., eds., *Urban Poverty in Africa*, London: IT Publications.

Rutherford, B., 2001, *Working on the Margins: Black Workers, White Farmers in Postcolonial Zimbabwe*, London/ Harare: Zed Books/Weaver Press.

Schlyter, A., 1999, 'Recycled Inequalities: Youth and Gender in the George Compound, Zambia', Uppsala: Nordiska Afrikainstitutet.

Stitcher, S., 1995, *Migrant Labour*, Cambridge: Cambridge University Press.

Ungar, S., 2001, 'Moral Panic versus Risk Society: The Implication of Changing Sites of Social Anxiety', in *British Journal of Sociology*, Vol. 52, No. 2, pp271-291.

Werbner, R., 1995, 'Human Rights and Moral Knowledge: Arguments of Accountability in Zimbabwe', in Strathern, M., ed., *Shifting Contexts: Transformation in Anthropological Knowledge*, London: Routledge.

Worby, E., 1994, 'Maps, Names and Ethnic Games: the Epistemology and Iconography of Colonial Power in Northwestern Zimbabwe', in *Journal of Southern African Studies*, Vol. 20, No. 3, pp 371-392.

www.ingramcontent.com/pod-product-compliance
Lightning Source LLC
Chambersburg PA
CBHW021611210326
41599CB00010B/707